Graphic Organizers in Social Studies™

Learning About America's Colonial Period with Graphic Organizers

Linda Wirkner

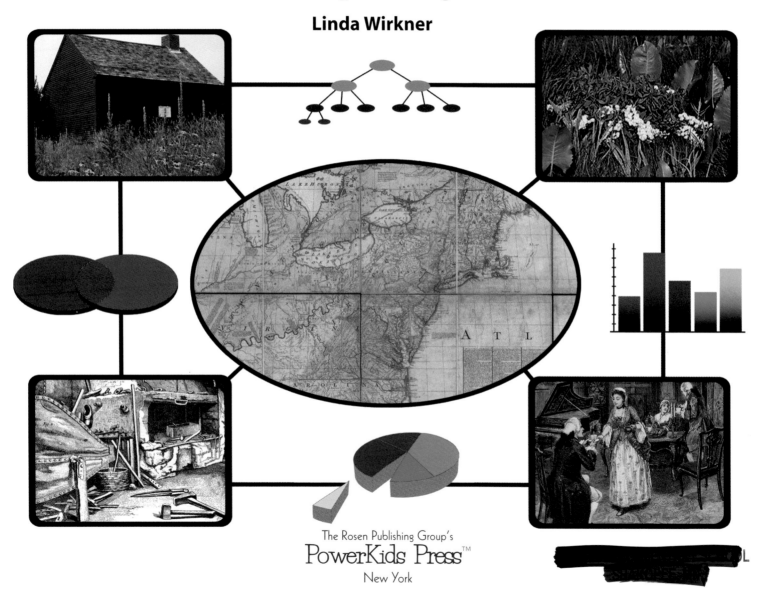

The Rosen Publishing Group's
PowerKids Press™
New York

For Frank Matotek, my wonderful father

Published in 2005 by The Rosen Publishing Group, Inc.
29 East 21st Street, New York, NY 10010

First Edition

Editor: Orli Zuravicky
Book Design: Michael Caroleo

Photo Credits: Cover and p. 1 (top left), p. 11 © Lee Snider; Lee Snider/CORBIS; cover and p. 1 (top right), p. 20 © Gerald D. Tang; cover and p. 1 (bottom right), pp. 7 (bottom right), 8 (top left), 15 © North Wind Pictures; cover and p. 1 (bottom left), p. 19 (both) © Dover Publications; cover and p. 1 (middle) Map Division Library of Congress; pp. 7 (bottom left), 16 (sage, rosemary, thyme) © Royalty-Free/ CORBIS; p. 16 (mint) © W. Cody/CORBIS; p. 16 (mullein) © Frank Young; Papilio/CORBIS; p. 16 (lavender) © Jacqui Hurst/CORBIS; p. 16 (basil) © Mark E. Gibson/CORBIS; p. 16 (aloe) © Tony Arruza/CORBIS.

Library of Congress Cataloging-in-Publication Data

Wirkner, Linda.
Learning about America's colonial period with graphic organizers / Linda Wirkner.
    p. cm. — (Graphic organizers in social studies)
Includes bibliographical references and index.
ISBN 1-4042-2811-X (Library Binding) — ISBN 1-4042-5052-2 (Paperback)
1. United States—History—Colonial period, ca. 1600–1775—Juvenile literature. 2. Graphic organizers—Juvenile literature. 3. United States—History—Colonial period, ca. 1600–1775—Study and teaching (Elementary) [1. United States—History—Colonial period, ca. 1600–1775.] I. Title.
E188.W62 2005
973.2—dc22
                          2003024799

Manufactured in the United States of America

Contents

America's Colonial Period 5

European Influences 6

The Thirteen Original Colonies 9

Lifestyles in the Colonies 10

Colonial Government 13

Colonial Americans 14

Colonial Remedies 17

Colonial Technology 18

Economy and Industry in the Colonies 21

Religion in the Colonies 22

Glossary 23

Index 24

Web Sites 24

Line Graph: Estimates of the Colonial Population from 1610 to 1800

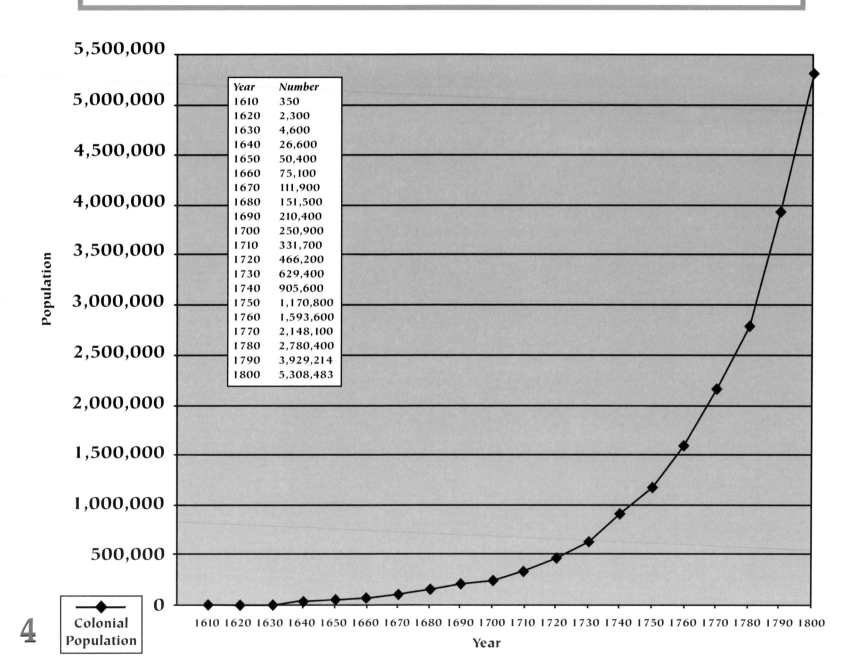

Year	Number
1610	350
1620	2,300
1630	4,600
1640	26,600
1650	50,400
1660	75,100
1670	111,900
1680	151,500
1690	210,400
1700	250,900
1710	331,700
1720	466,200
1730	629,400
1740	905,600
1750	1,170,800
1760	1,593,600
1770	2,148,100
1780	2,780,400
1790	3,929,214
1800	5,308,483

Population

Year

Colonial Population

4

America's Colonial Period

By 1733, there were 13 British colonies in America. Most of the European settlers who had come to America years before had stayed in the colonies. People from many different countries continued to come to live in America. America's population quickly increased. In the beginning of the **colonial period**, colonists were separated by differences in **culture** and **religion**. They struggled to stay connected to their homelands while trying to succeed in the **New World**. The colonial period ended with the creation of a new American culture, and a people who were willing to fight together for their new homeland. Colonists began to establish American **industries** and to build American cities.

Graphic organizers are tools that help you group different kinds of facts. This book will use these tools to help you learn about life in America's colonial period.

This line graph shows estimates, or educated guesses, of the change in colonial population over a period of time. The numbers at the bottom of the graph stand for years, and the ones on the left side stand for the population. As you can see, the population had greatly increased by 1800.

European Influences

European **influences** from early settlers can be found in much of today's American culture. The Dutch, who settled mostly in present-day New York in the early 1600s, began the practice of using the wind to power mills. They brought foods to America, such as tomatoes, lettuce, waffles, and doughnuts, which are still eaten today. The most well known Swedish addition to American culture is the log cabin, which appeared throughout the colonies. The Germans, who first settled in Pennsylvania in the late 1600s, brought the **custom** of decorating Christmas trees to America. The English influenced America most strongly, and their effect was long lasting. For example, the official language spoken in America is English. It is also said that the U.S. Constitution, the set of laws by which America is governed, was modeled after England's set of laws, called the Magna Carta.

This Venn diagram shows two circles overlapping. Each circle stands for a group of people and their views. The part where the circles overlap stands for the views that the subjects in the two circles share. It shows the similarities and differences between the British and American governments.

Venn Diagram: British Government and U.S. Government

British Government

- Government was ruled by a king, or monarch, who came to power because he belonged to a royal family
- King ruled for life
- Body of government was the monarch and Parliament, made up of two houses, the House of Lords and the House of Commons
- What Parliament and the king said was law

- Limited ruler's power
- Written down, not passed down by mouth
- The right to a fast, fair trial
- The right to a jury of regular citizens
- The right to protection against harsh punishment
- The right for the people to have representation in the government
- The right to vote on taxation
- The idea of a Bill of Rights for the people's human rights

U.S. Government

- People elected a ruler, called a president
- The president serves for a fixed amount of time
- Has three different bodies of government, they are the legislative, the executive, and the judicial branches
- Legislative branch made up of two houses, the Senate and the House of Representatives
- Constitution can be amended, or changed, if enough people vote to change it

The log cabin in this photograph is much like old-fashioned colonial cabins. In colonial times, families of 10 or more lived in one cabin together!

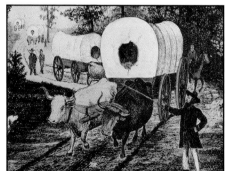

German colonists invented the Conestoga wagon. These wagons were used by settlers when they traveled West in the early 1800s.

7

Map: New England, Middle, and Southern Colonies

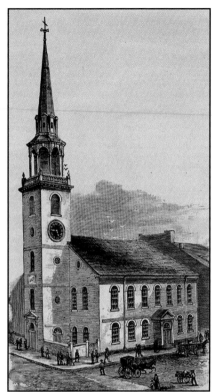

This is a print of the Old South Meeting House in Boston, Massachusetts. In colonial times, most town activities centered around the town meetinghouse, or church. The Old South Meeting House was where colonists met to plan the Boston Tea Party in 1773.

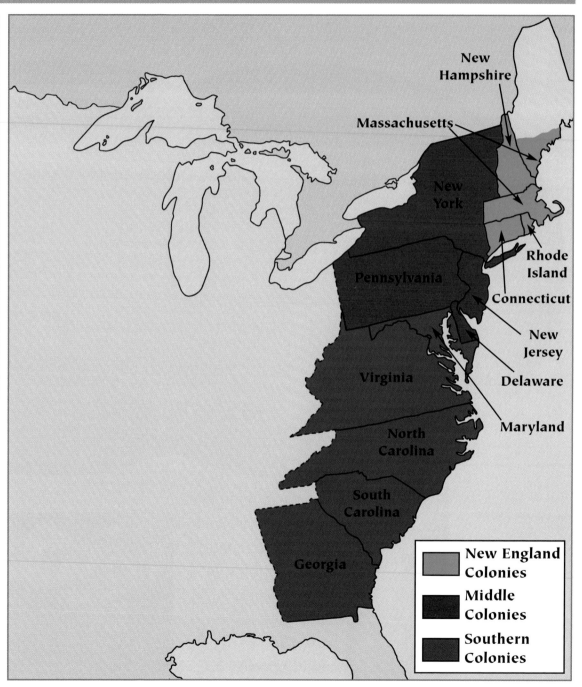

New Hampshire

Massachusetts

New York

Rhode Island

Connecticut

Pennsylvania

New Jersey

Delaware

Virginia

Maryland

North Carolina

South Carolina

Georgia

New England Colonies

Middle Colonies

Southern Colonies

The Thirteen Original Colonies

The colonies became known as New England colonies, middle colonies, and southern colonies based on their location. The New England colonies included Massachusetts, New Hampshire, Connecticut, and Rhode Island. New England towns were small. Houses, churches, and schools were grouped close together. Nearby farms provided food locally, but the stony landscape could not produce good crops. The middle colonies were New York, New Jersey, Pennsylvania, and Delaware. The middle colonies were home to two of the biggest and busiest cities, New York City and Philadelphia. Most governing and business took place in the middle colonies. The southern colonies were North Carolina, South Carolina, Virginia, Maryland, and Georgia. Southern land was plentiful and fruitful. Plantations, or large farms, were spread far apart from one another.

A map is a way to study different places and their locations. The map to the left shows the original 13 colonies. The colors on the map show which colonies were New England, which colonies were middle, and which colonies were southern.

Lifestyles in the Colonies

Most New Englanders in colonial times were Puritan, so their lives centered around the church. Houses and public buildings were also built around the church. Community leaders played a big role in daily life. The people of the middle colonies had many religions and cultures. The middle colonies were less focused on religion and more interested in education, trade, and government. The southern colonists based their lifestyle around their plantations. People who worked on the plantations also lived there. Plantations included buildings for jobs such as sewing and **carpentry**, which were necessary to run the plantation. New England colonists and middle colonists thought that education was very important. Most of their children went to school to learn how to read and write. Southern children were usually schooled in their homes. Southern children were expected to follow in their parents' footsteps.

The graphic organizer to the right is a compare/contrast chart. It shows the different aspects, or features, of certain subjects and compares them to each other. This chart compares and contrasts life in all three groups of colonies.

Compare/Contrast Chart: The New England, Middle, and Southern Colonies

	New England Colonies	Middle Colonies	Southern Colonies
Main Religions	Most New Englanders were Puritans.	The people of the middle colonies followed many different religions.	Most colonists in the southern colonies were Anglicans.
Reasons for Establishing a Colony	The first colonists who came to New England were looking for a place where they could have religious freedom.	Dutch settlers came to the middle colonies for trade purposes, and to make money. They had no real interest in creating a settlement. Later on, the English took the land from the Dutch for settlements.	Colonists came to the southern colonies for two main reasons, to make money and to provide Britain with new trade markets.
Economy	The economy was based heavily on furniture making, especially chairs. Fishing and shipbuilding were also major industries.	The economy was based on trading fur and wood. The wood was used for building houses, furniture, and industry.	The economy was based largely on plantation farming. The main crops were tobacco, rice, indigo, and wine grapes.
Education	Education was important to the New England colonists. They opened the first libraries and schools in the colonies. They were the first to offer higher education by establishing some of the first colleges, Harvard and Yale, which still exist today.	They were the first colonies to pass a law that said that every town had to have a grammar school. Schools in the middle colonies were mainly religious in nature. They taught other subjects as well so that the students could get into college.	They had tutors mainly from Ireland and Scotland to teach their children. Most people were not interested in public education.

This is a photograph of the Nathan Hale Schoolhouse, located in East Haddam, Connecticut. Education in colonial times was different from education today. Schools at that time were simply one-room houses like this one. Nathan Hale taught here from 1773 to 1774.

Chart: Colonial Governments

Type of Colony	Government Role	Appointed By	Job
Royal/Proprietary	Governor	The king of England or the proprietor	Stood for the Crown, but had some responsibility to the people, could call to order or close any meeting of the houses, could veto any of their laws, and could appoint all colonial officials.
Royal/Proprietary	Lower House: Assembly	The people of the colony voted (in Massachusetts, the Upper House chose the Lower House)	Had the right to tax the colonists, control money, control officials' salaries, and create laws, but laws could be vetoed by the governor. For royal colonies, laws had to be approved by the king.
Royal/Proprietary	Upper House: Council	The king of England or the proprietor	There to advise the governor, act as the Upper House, take part in the lawmaking, and act as a high court.
Self-Governing	Governor	The people of the colony	Governor had no responsibility to the king of England. Oversaw the colony, stood for the people, could call together both houses and veto laws.
Self-Governing	Lower House: Assembly	The people of the colony	Right to tax the colonists, control money, and create laws, but the laws had to be passed by the council as well as by the governor.
Self-Governing	Upper House: Council	The people of the colony	Both advised the governor and acted as the colony's court.

Colonial Government

The colonies were officially governed by the king of England. However, there was still a need for local governments. There were three types of colonies in the New World. Royal colonies had governors who were appointed by the king of England. Before royal colonies could pass a new law, it had to be sent across the ocean to England for the king's **approval**. **Proprietary** colonies were established by wealthy men who were given land by the king. These men chose their colony's governor. Self-governing colonies were founded by colonists. They chose their own government leaders. Most colonies had a governor, a **council**, and an **assembly**, which approved colonial laws. These colonial governments were the foundation for America's government today. Colonists came to America looking for freedom. They wanted a voice in making the laws under which they lived.

A chart lists different facts about connected subjects. This chart separates the colonies into royal, self-governing, and proprietary governments. It then lists the major governing bodies in each type of government, and shows what their jobs were in each type of colony.

Colonial Americans

Colonists were separated into different social groups. One's social class played a big role in deciding one's job, lawful rights, and influence in colonial government. Some colonists were part of the upper class, or gentry. These colonists were well educated and wealthy. Some gentry owned southern plantations, some were doctors, and some held leadership positions. Middle-class colonists were less wealthy than the gentry, but they still held respectable positions in the community. Middle-class colonists owned small farms and businesses. They worked in skilled crafts such as shoemaking and cabinetmaking. Middle-class men could vote and hold small government jobs. The colonial lower class included servants, slaves, regular workers, and apprentices, or people studying to learn a trade. These colonists usually could not read, write, or afford to own land. Therefore, they could not vote.

A classifying web separates people or places into different categories, or groups. This web shows the three different social classes in colonial America. It also shows the different types of clothing that were worn by each class, and what types of jobs members of each class could hold.

Classifying Web: Colonial Social Classes

Colonial Social Classes

The Upper Class

Clothing

The wealthiest colonists wore fine linen, silk, velvet, satin, and cotton fabrics. Many of these fabrics were brought from Europe. They wore fashionable wigs and caps with turned-up rims. Their outfits were decorated with lace, silver buckles, expensive buttons, jewelry, and silk. They had fans, handbags, and gloves, as well.

Jobs

Upper-class colonists owned big plantations. They were merchants, doctors, ministers, and lawyers. They also held leadership positions, were colonial officials, and were members of the assembly.

The Middle Class

Clothing

Middle-class colonists wore wool and linen. They wore simple leather shoes and knit stockings. Some wore wigs and fine fabrics, but they were less fancy than those of the upper class. Laborers wore caps.

Jobs

Middle-class colonists owned small farms, shops, and businesses. They were skilled dressmakers, shoemakers, and carpenters. Some men held small government jobs as well.

The Lower Class

Clothing

The lower class went barefoot often, or they wore very simple shoes or sandals. They wore clothes made of homemade cloth and linen. They wore straw hats for shade in the field.

Jobs

Lower-class colonists were field workers, servants, and slaves. Sailors were also members of this class, as were apprentices and shop workers.

This hand-colored woodcut shows upper-class colonists drinking tea. Only the richest colonists could afford the fine lace and silk to make this dress. If you look closely, you can see the silver buckle on the woman's shoe.

15

Concept Web: Colonial Herb Garden

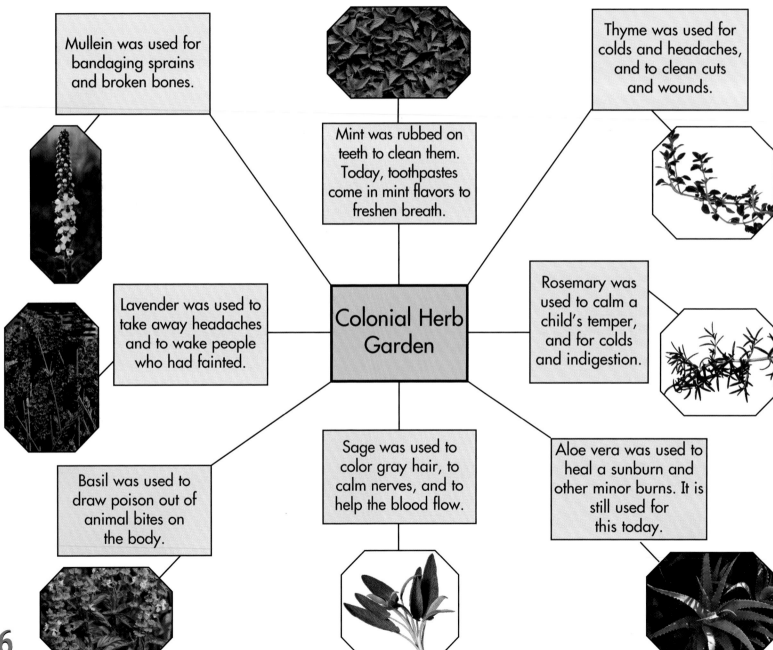

Mullein was used for bandaging sprains and broken bones.

Mint was rubbed on teeth to clean them. Today, toothpastes come in mint flavors to freshen breath.

Thyme was used for colds and headaches, and to clean cuts and wounds.

Lavender was used to take away headaches and to wake people who had fainted.

Colonial Herb Garden

Rosemary was used to calm a child's temper, and for colds and indigestion.

Basil was used to draw poison out of animal bites on the body.

Sage was used to color gray hair, to calm nerves, and to help the blood flow.

Aloe vera was used to heal a sunburn and other minor burns. It is still used for this today.

Colonial Remedies

Colonial doctors did not know much about **diseases** or the human body. Most doctors believed that illnesses were caused by an imbalance in the body's **fluids**, such as water or blood. They believed that the "bad" fluid needed to be removed. They put leeches, which are wormlike creatures, on the sick person's body to suck it out. There were not many doctors in the colonies and most colonists could not afford their services. Often the woman of the house was put in charge of her family's healthcare. Nearly every house had an **herb** garden. Women mixed different herbs to create homemade remedies, or drugs, for all types of illnesses. Sometimes these remedies worked. More often they did not. During colonial times, thousands of colonists and Native Americans died from diseases because doctors and people had neither the knowledge nor the ability to heal them.

The graphic organizer to the left is called a concept web. The main idea is in the center, and all of the other ideas are connected to the central idea. This concept web shows the different types of herbs that were grown in colonial gardens and what each herb was used for.

Colonial Technology

Life in the colonies was hard. People tried to improve **technology** by creating tools to help them with daily life. They made important improvements to their rifles, or guns. Colonists depended on hunting for much of their food. European rifles were slow and heavy. By the mid-1700s, colonists had found ways to make their rifles lighter, longer, faster, and more exact. They also made lighter **ammunition**. Another colonial invention was made by Oliver Evans, of Delaware. A tool called a card was used to comb sheep's wool, so that it could be spun into yarn. Making the teeth for the comb was tiring and slow. Evans created a machine that could make 1,500 teeth per minute! This machine allowed colonists to produce more yarn for cloth. Over the years, the colonists improved tools for all of their trades. Many of these tools are still in use today, such as the hammer.

This graphic organizer is a chart. Charts explain different facts about connected subjects. The left-hand column lists the different kinds of tools that were used in colonial times. The middle column lists which trades used which tools, and the last column explains what the tools were used for.

Chart: Tools Used in Colonial Trades

Tools	Trade	Use
Hammer	Carpentry, blacksmithing, and silversmithing	This was used to drive nails in and to pull them out.
Mallet	Carpentry and cabinetmaking	This was used to drive nails into surfaces that metal would damage.
Plane	Carpentry	This blade was used to help cut at the correct angle, depth, and position.
Anvil	Blacksmithing, silversmithing, and brass founding	This metal block was used as a surface on which to pound.
Forge	Blacksmithing, brass founding, and silversmithing	This box with an opening for air acts as a fireplace. It is used to heat metal.
Gimlet	Carpentry	This was used to drill holes for small nails.

This is an engraving of a blacksmith's forge. A forge was a large, open oven that blacksmiths used for heating and melting metal and iron. After the metal was hot enough to bend, the blacksmith would shape it by hammering it on the anvil.

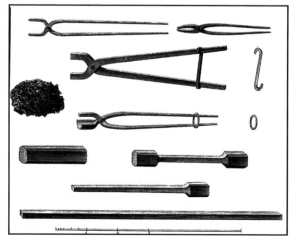

This engraving shows some of the tools that the blacksmith used in colonial times.

19

Sequence Chart: Making Indigo Dye

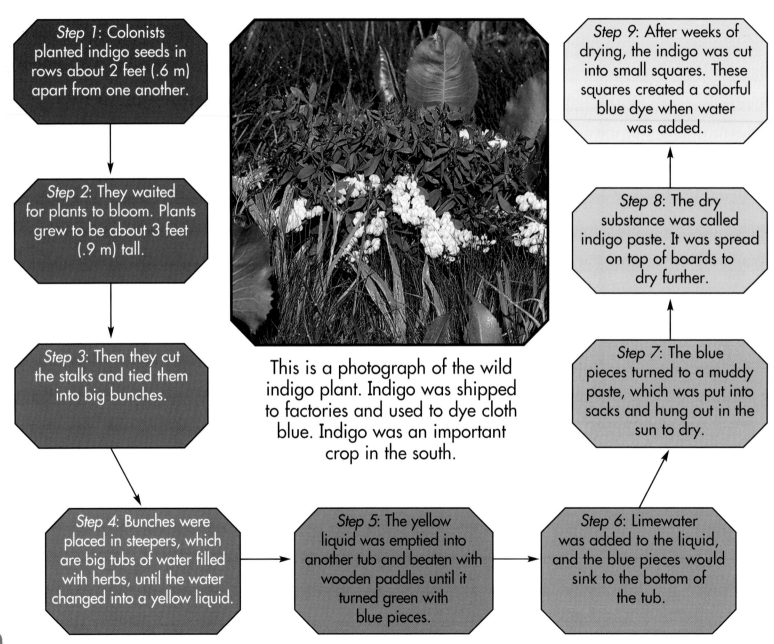

Step 1: Colonists planted indigo seeds in rows about 2 feet (.6 m) apart from one another.

Step 2: They waited for plants to bloom. Plants grew to be about 3 feet (.9 m) tall.

Step 3: Then they cut the stalks and tied them into big bunches.

This is a photograph of the wild indigo plant. Indigo was shipped to factories and used to dye cloth blue. Indigo was an important crop in the south.

Step 9: After weeks of drying, the indigo was cut into small squares. These squares created a colorful blue dye when water was added.

Step 8: The dry substance was called indigo paste. It was spread on top of boards to dry further.

Step 7: The blue pieces turned to a muddy paste, which was put into sacks and hung out in the sun to dry.

Step 4: Bunches were placed in steepers, which are big tubs of water filled with herbs, until the water changed into a yellow liquid.

Step 5: The yellow liquid was emptied into another tub and beaten with wooden paddles until it turned green with blue pieces.

Step 6: Limewater was added to the liquid, and the blue pieces would sink to the bottom of the tub.

Economy and Industry in the Colonies

Colonists had to figure out how to create a good **economy** in their colony. If a colony lacked rich soil for farming, the colonists had to build an economy around other industries. New England's Atlantic coast was plentiful with fish, creating a successful fishing industry. New England also had thick forests. New England colonists traded lumber for goods that they lacked. They also used lumber in their growing shipbuilding industry. The good soil in Pennsylvania, New Jersey, and New York enabled these middle colonies to grow wheat and other grains, which they **exported**. Fur trading was another big industry. New York's harbor became a major shipping port. Rich soil, flat land, and warm weather allowed southern colonies to start large plantations. They grew tobacco, indigo, rice, and cotton. Southerners grew enough crops for their own livelihood as well as for trade with Europe.

This graphic organizer is a sequence chart. A sequence chart explains the order of steps in a process or event that has a beginning and an end. This sequence chart shows the process for making indigo dye, a product that was very successful for the southern economy.

Religion in the Colonies

As early as 1680, New York City was filled with people from many different religions. These included **Anglicans**, Quakers, Puritans, and Jews. The lives of the Puritans, who lived all over New England, were ruled by their religion. Anglicans, who lived mostly in the South, combined religious and social events. They saw these events as chances to gather as a community. The Quakers of Pennsylvania welcomed people of all faiths and believed in peace and respect for their fellow man. In the 1740s, a religious movement called the Great Awakening swept across the colonies, highlighting the importance of religion in life. Although religion played a major role in founding the colonies, over the years its role lessened. What remained was the **foundation** for freedom and equal rights. Colonists had come to the colonies for freedoms they could not find elsewhere, and these are the ideals upon which America was built.

Glossary

ammunition (am-yoo-NIH-shun) Things fired from weapons, such as bullets.

Anglicans (AN-glih-kenz) Followers of a religion based on the laws of the Church of England.

approval (uh-PROO-vul) Allowance.

assembly (uh-SEM-blee) A group of people who meet to advise a government.

carpentry (KAR-pun-tree) The act of making something out of wood.

colonial period (kuh-LOH-nee-ul PIR-ee-id) The time in history when the United States was made up of thirteen colonies that were ruled by England.

council (KOWN-sul) A group called together to discuss or settle questions.

culture (KUL-chur) The beliefs, practices, and arts of a group of people.

custom (KUS-tum) A practice common to many people in an area or a social class.

diseases (duh-ZEEZ-ez) Illnesses or sicknesses.

economy (ih-KAH-nuh-mee) The way in which a country or a business manages its supplies and energy sources.

exported (EK-sport-ed) Sent to another place or land to be sold.

fluids (FLOO-idz) Liquids.

foundation (fown-DAY-shun) The part on which other parts are built.

graphic organizers (GRA-fik OR-guh-ny-zerz) Charts, graphs, and pictures that sort facts and ideas and make them clear.

herb (ERB) A plant used for medicine or for seasoning food.

industries (IN-dus-treez) Businesses in which many people work and make money producing a certain product.

influences (IN-floo-ens-ez) Things that sway others without using force.

New World (NOO WURLD) North America and South America.

proprietary (pruh-PRY-uh-tehr-ee) Privately owned or managed.

religion (ree-LIH-jen) A belief in and a way of worshipping a god or gods.

technology (tek-NAH-luh-jee) The way that a people do something using tools, and the tools that they use.

Index

A
ammunition, 18

C
Christmas tree, 6
culture(s), 5–6, 10

D
diseases, 17
doctors, 14, 17

E
economy, 21
education, 10

F
fishing, 21
fur trading, 21

G
governors, 13
graphic organizers, 5
Great Awakening, 22

H
herb garden, 17

I
industries, 5, 21

M
Magna Carta, 6

N
New World, 5, 13

P
plantations, 9–10, 14, 21
proprietary colonies, 13

R
religion(s), 5, 10, 22
rifles, 18
royal colonies, 13

S
self-governing colonies, 13
shipbuilding, 21
social class, 14

T
technology, 18

U
U.S. Constitution, 6

Web Sites

Due to the changing nature of Internet links, PowerKids Press has developed an online list of Web sites related to the subject of this book. This site is updated regularly. Please use this link to access the list:
www.powerkidslinks.com/goss/colonialp/